Assert Yourself

**This book offers a short do-it-yourself course in
Assertiveness Training for men and women,
both as individuals and in groups.**

About the Author

Gael Lindenfield is a freelance psychotherapist who leads her own personal development consultancy, running courses for individuals, groups and organizations in England and Southern Spain. Throughout her career she has been a pioneering force in the self-help movement, initiating and running many innovative and successful projects for both statutory and voluntary mental health organizations. She has developed her own blend of creative and behavioural techniques which have proved highly successful in helping people to improve their self-confidence and break persistent negative habits. Through her writing and work with the media, she is also committed to making these exciting personal development opportunities accessible to millions of other people who may be looking for ways to change themselves and their lives.

She is the author of SUPER CONFIDENCE, THE POSITIVE WOMAN, MANAGING ANGER, CONFIDENT CHILDREN, SELF MOTIVATION and SELF ESTEEM.

ASSERT YOURSELF

A self-help assertiveness
programme for men and women

Gael Lindenfield

Thorsons

Thorsons
An Imprint of HarperCollins*Publishers*
77–85 Fulham Palace Road
Hammersmith, London W6 8JB

Published by Thorsons 1992

15 17 18 16

© Gael Lindenfield 1986

Gael Lindenfield asserts the moral right to
be identified as the author of this work

A catalogue record for this book
is available from the British Library

ISBN 0 7225 2652 0

Typeset by Harper Phototypesetters Limited,
Northampton, England
Printed and bound in Great Britain by
Clays Ltd, St Ives plc

All rights reserved. No part of this publication may be
reproduced, stored in a retrieval system, or transmitted,
in any form or by any means, electronic, mechanical,
photocopying, recording or otherwise, without the prior
permission of the publishers.

Dedication

To my daughters, Susie and Laura,
who have taught me so much about
assertiveness.

Contents

Be Assertive

Compromise — only if it's reasonable to do so

Open — and be honest

Negotiate — firmly and wisely

Fair — to you as well as others!

Innovate — don't wait for others — or fate

Direct — and clear in your speech

Expressive — show your feelings when appropriate

Non-verbal — use your body and beware of hidden messages

Chance — take risks

Empower — everyone!

Acknowledgements

Most importantly, I would like to thank all the people who have attended my courses and given me such helpful and constructive feedback.

I would also like to thank Robert Adams for so willingly helping me to prepare the final text for publication.

Finally, I must thank my husband in his constant encouragement and challenge to my own assertiveness!

Introduction

This book is based on an Assertiveness Training Programme I have used with a variety of groups during the past six years. It is, by no means, a definitive model either for myself or anyone else. It can and should be adapted, abridged, expanded — or indeed abandoned according to your own individual needs. In writing it, I have aimed to provide the following:—

1. A Concise, Simple Account of the Theory and Principles

— as they are applicable to both men and women living within our Western culture.

Much of Assertiveness Training is concerned with changing or adapting our values, ideas and philosophy. Often we are unassertive merely because we think that it is wrong to be assertive. These thoughts may be quite deeply rooted in our minds as they are often placed there in early childhood and are embedded in the values of our culture. Our first task must, therefore, be to 'reprogramme' our minds by replacing the old unassertive values and thoughts with a more positive philosophy. From my own

13

personal experience and the experience of people on my courses it seems that the repetition of appropriate quotations and proverbs is a useful way of effecting this change.

Throughout the book you will notice a number of these quotes and proverbs. They have been written in italics so that they can be easily identified and used as an occasional reminder of the philosophy of assertiveness. In my groups, I often write out some on large wall posters and suggest that this can be done at home or in the office as well.

I appreciate that some people might find them an irritating distraction from the text. If this should happen please ignore them and read on!

2.   A Manual for Self-Help Groups

Assertiveness Training is most often undertaken in a group situation. After all, old habits certainly do die hard but they do seem to vanish more quickly when we receive support and encouragement from others who can understand what the battle is all about.

Part II of this book offers a programme of exercises which could be completed in approximately 8 weekly sessions of 2 hours each. The appropriate theory can be introduced in the form of posters and handouts derived from the text in Part I.

By using this book as a manual, the responsibility for leading the group could be shared by some or all of the participants.

A new inexperienced group might find one earlier publication helpful ('*Problem Solving Through Self-Help Groups*' by Gael Lindenfield and Robert Adams, Self-Help Associates, 1984).

3. A Manual for Individuals

If for some reason you are unable, or unwilling, to join a self-help group, this basic programme can be adapted for use on your own at home.

At the end of each practical exercise I have made some suggestions about how you could achieve this. I suggest, as with self-help groups, you could work on one short session each week over a period of 2 months. It is important to cover the basic ground very thoroughly and not to try too much too quickly. You may need more self-discipline and motivation to work in this way, but it should still be possible to make some effective progress.

One final note — on reading this book, you may notice that although it is addressed to both men and women, I have used the pronoun 'he' rather than 'she' throughout.

As I personally do not like constantly reading 'he or she' in a book, I was faced with making a choice. My choice was influenced by the fact that, fortunately, there already appears to be a growing awareness of the need for women to adopt more assertive styles of behaviour. Men, on the other hand, have only recently recognized how useful Assertiveness Training can be to them.

When I first started running courses six years ago, it was very rare for men to be amongst the participants. Nowadays, we certainly have as many requests for help from men as we do from women.

Part 1
Ideas and Theory of Assertiveness Training

Chapter 1

Arguments for Assertiveness

What is Assertiveness?

The word assertiveness is used to describe a certain kind of behaviour. It is behaviour which helps us to communicate clearly and confidently our NEEDS, WANTS and FEELINGS to other people without abusing in any way their human rights. It is an alternative to passive, aggressive and manipulative behaviour.

If we want to be assertive we must:

- Decide what we want.
- Decide if it is fair.
- Ask clearly for it.
- Not be afraid of taking risks.
- Be calm and relaxed.
- Express our feelings openly.
- Give and take compliments easily.
- Give and take fair criticism.

We must not:

- Beat about the bush.
- Go behind people's backs.
- Bully.

- Call people names.
- Bottle up our feelings.

Very few people manage to be assertive in all areas of their life. Some of us manage to be assertive at home but have difficulties at work. Others may be fine when they are working but are unable to assert themselves within their personal relationships.

Why Are We Unassertive?

The child is Father to the man. Wordsworth

Those of us who are parents will remember only too well how little fear our new-born babies had about communicating their needs and feelings in an open and direct manner! As babies they may not have acquired the more sophisticated assertive skills of judging whether their demands are fair, or making requests in a calm relaxed manner, but they certainly do not beat about the bush!

Very quickly, however, children learn to adapt their behaviour according to the kind of response their requests receive. They may learn that by behaving as a good, quiet, sweet little child they get the goodies that they need or want. Alternatively, they may find that shouting, screaming and kicking brings a quicker and more satisfying response.

At school, children also go through the same unconscious learning process. There, they may find that the behaviour that worked best at home does not get the same results at school. They begin to experiment with different approaches and responses. I can remember still the feeling of astonishment I had when I went to my first Parents' Interview evening at my daughter's school. The quietly spoken, shy little girl that the teacher was describing seemed so amazingly different from the lively,

20

noisy toddler I had known at home for the last few years!

This process of learning to adapt our behaviour to suit different social relationships is easier for some of us than others. Much will depend on how successful and satisfying our relationships with the most important figures in our life have been.

If our demands for physical and emotional nourishment from our parents or parent substitutes were well met – we will find the process of adapting our behaviour to different situations relatively easy. If our early basic demands were not well satisified – we will try again elsewhere. Unfortunately, we may try in the most inappropriate places and end up getting rejected. For example, a child who tries to get his basic needs fulfilled at school may well get rebuffed and punished for being 'attention-seeking', 'clingy' or 'over-anxious to please'.

In our sophisticated Western society, we generally cater for the physical needs of children reasonably well. Catering adequately for their emotional needs on the other hand, is often not so easily achieved.

If we wish our children to grow up into confident, assertive adults, we will need to provide them with the following:

a **model of assertive behaviour** – someone who is assertive with them and whom they trust and respect and will want to be like.

love and encouragement – to build up a sense of their own worth.

caring criticism – to enable them to see themselves, their actions, and their demands realistically.

a **sense of values** – to help them assess their own and others' rights.

a **basic feeling of security** – to enable them to experiment with risks and make mistakes.

This is, of course, a very tall order which very few of us can meet. We can take comfort from this proverb:

He that hath no children brings them up well.

Of course it isn't only the influence of our parents that we must examine in order to find the cause of our unassertive behaviour. There are many other factors to take into consideration such as:

● **our position in the family** – were we the first, middle or last child?

● **the influence of other relatives**, such as big sisters or brothers.

● **what sort of school did we go to** and how did we get on with the teachers and other children?

● **what did we achieve** at school and later at work?

● **our sex** – in our society women tend to be passive while men are often aggressive.

● **our social class** – sometimes money and power make it easier for us to be more assertive though unfortunately they also seem to encourage aggressive behaviour.

Assertiveness Training does not strictly speaking concern itself with the causes of problems but rather with the development of appropriate skills to cope with them. In my groups, however, I am finding it more and more helpful to spend some time looking at this question.

Before coming on a course, unassertive people are so busy blaming themselves for being so inadequate that they haven't given a thought as to how their personal and social background might have affected their behaviour. A little understanding of how we become unassertive can help reduce the feelings of guilt and give your self-esteem and motivation a boost.

Many centuries ago Virgil came to this same conclusion!

> *Happy is he who has been able to learn the cause of things.*
>
> Virgil

Why Bother to be Assertive?

> *When the fight begins within himself the man is worth something.*
>
> Robert Browning

It is important at the start of any Assertiveness Training programme to be very clear about both the advantages and disadvantages of becoming more assertive.

Most people register on my courses because they hope that if they learn to be more assertive, they will get more of what they want. Unfortunately, this is not always true.

Assertiveness Training helps us to communicate our needs more openly and honestly but it cannot guarantee that they will be met. Assertive behaviour more often leads to compromise and negotiation rather than an outright win for one party. Often, manipulative, 'behind the back' techniques and aggressive behaviour actually gets us more of what we want in terms of material goods or power. It does so, though, often at great expense to our personal relationships and self-esteem. Biographies of very many powerful and successful people reveal loneliness and feelings of self-deprecation.

Assertiveness Training teaches us to behave in such a way so that we do not continually come away from situations feeling bad about ourselves. We will come away with the satisfaction that we 'did our best' and did not abuse the rights of others.

The good news is that people who are generally assertive are confident and relaxed people who are happy simply to be themselves.

> *Best be yourself, imperial, plain and true*
> **Robert Browning**

Assertive people are aware both of their strengths and their weaknesses. They are not afraid of taking risks and know that by doing so, they will probably make many mistakes.

> *Experience is the name everyone gives to their mistakes.*
> **Oscar Wilde**

If you are assertive you will view mistakes positively and see them as an opportunity to learn and do better next time. You will have learned to gauge your successes by your own capabilities and potential rather than by continually comparing yourself with other people. Accepting your own capabilities will help you to set yourself realistic goals so that you do not continually put yourself into situations where you will feel a failure.

Being assertive also means accepting that not everyone in the world will be kind and caring towards you. You will develop the ability to spot when you are being abused or 'put down' and you will know how to cope with unfair criticism and exploitation.

Finally, you will learn to use assertiveness **appropriately**. You will be aware that there are some situations when it is wise to take a back seat and some where it is appropriate to fight for your, and others', rights. An obvious example of when assertive behaviour might not be appropriate would be when you or others are in physical danger.

Yes, certainly learning to be assertive is worth the effort. Even the process of learning the skills can be challenging and fun.

Change brings life. Proverb

An Assertiveness Training group may be exhausting but most people find the supportive, caring and often humorous atmosphere a wonderful experience. They treasure the unique opportunity to be completely open about their strengths and weaknesses and help each other work constructively on their problems.

The support you can get in an Assertiveness Training group can help you to cope with the inevitable changes in your life and relationships. For some people these changes may take place very smoothly but for others the period of transition can be very stressful.

It is not uncommon for many people at the end of an Assertiveness Training course to feel dissatisfied with some of their previous relationships. As they become more assertive they realize how suffocating these relationships have been and unless the other person is willing to change or adapt, a parting of the ways often results.

The period between ending a friendship and finding a more satisfying replacement can be unsettling. This is when you will find invaluable the support of 'true friends' and your group.

We are so fond of one another because our ailments are the same.

Jonathan Swift

Chapter 2

The Essence of Assertiveness

What is the Difference Between Aggression, Passivity and Assertion?

Every person at some time has to cope with a problem. I have always found it very useful to spend a considerable amount of time helping people to distinguish between three ways of behaving when they are facing a problem.

Two basic instinctual responses when encountering a problem are **Flight** (passivity) and **Fight** (aggression). Many mental health and relationship problems are caused by an over-reliance on these two basic animal responses.

Man, however, has developed a third response more suited to the solving of the kind of relationship problems he has encountered through community living. This response involves the use of his more sophisticated brain and verbal skills. It is his ability to **Discuss**, **Argue** and **Negotiate**.

Assertiveness Training aims to help us develop the third response which is often a more appropriate and successful way of communicating with our fellow men and women.

There is a growing awareness in our society of the pitfalls of aggression and passivity and such behaviours are now often considered socially unacceptable. Unfortunately, this does not necessarily mean that these behaviours are used less frequently but rather that they are more heavily disguised and less easy to distinguish.

How often we are all fooled by the person who is 'all talk and no action' – or the 'charming' person who always manages to make us feel small and useless in their company.

Many people are confused about the different behaviours and are unassertive simply because they are afraid to be seen as passive or aggressive. Once again, 'the need to be liked' may be getting in the way of them standing up for their own rights.

> *How I like to be liked, and what I do to be liked!*
> **Charles Lamb**

The following chart can be used for a quick reference throughout your Assertiveness Training programme.

The Three Behaviours

Aggressive	Passive	Assertive
Non-Verbal Signals		
Shouting	Whining voice	Calm and controlled voice
Loud voice	Clenched, wringing hands	Relaxed posture
Pointing finger	Shuffling feet	Direct eye contact
Folded arms	Downcast eyes	Upright
Still posture	Stoop	
Key Words And Sentences – Used With the Appropriate Non-Verbal Behaviour		
You'd better	Maybe	I

Aggressive	Passive	Assertive
. . . If you don't	I guess	I think
Watch out.	I wonder	I feel
Come on	Would you mind very much if . . .	I want
Should	Sorry . . . sorry . . . sorry	Let's
Bad	Excuse me, please	How can we resolve this?
Stupid!	But	What do you think?
You!	You know	What do you see?
	If	
	I hope you don't mind	

'. . . The "charming" person who always manages to make us feel small.'

Assessing Your Problems

Discontent is the first step in progress. Proverb

When people first decide to do something about their under-assertiveness, they are usually motivated because they want to solve one or two major problems in their life. This may be a rather complex difficulty in relating to a member of their family, a boss or a colleague. Most people will, naturally, be very anxious about these problems and will want to talk about them frequently.

Initially it is important to have a chance to air these problems but for the purposes of a basic Assertiveness Training programme I suggest that everyone put these major worries firmly aside. In the first instance, all energy should be focused on smaller and more manageable difficulties.

Starting with the small problem means that we are not having to battle with the crippling anxiety that surrounds the major issues and, therefore, we have more of a chance to succeed and have immediate rewards.

He that corrects not small faults will not control great ones. Proverb

In Assertiveness Training we use some of the basic principles of **Behaviour Change Theory**. Psychologists have found that the most effective way of learning any new skill or behaviour is to:

- ensure that the learner is calm and relaxed when trying out the new behaviour (**anxiety reduction**).
- ensure that the learner is rewarded as soon as possible for any observable achievement (**positive reinforcement**).

'. . . Starting with the small problems.'

Firstly –
   We must **Identify** our problems

And secondly –
   We must **Grade** them in order of importance.

The following check lists can be used either as posters for the group to work from or they can be adapted to produce individual question and answer worksheets.

Possible Problem Areas

Am I able to . . .	Examples
Express positive feelings?	I like your coat. I think you did a really good job today. I love you. I'm happy today.
Express negative feelings?	I didn't like the way you did that . . . I much prefer the natural colour of your hair. I'm scared. I feel really miserable today.
Refuse requests and invitations?	No, I can't work late tonight. No, I don't like that kind of film, music, etc. No, I don't wish to get involved. No, I can't help you today – or ever! No, I don't want to make love tonight.
Express personal opinion?	I think the meeting has gone on long enough. I disagree with . . . I think . . .
Express justified anger?	You are late again – I feel angry. I feel really irritated when you . . .

Personal Problem Profile

People

Using the above chart as a check, list any problems you have with the following people:

- Friends of the same sex.
- Friends of the opposite sex.
- Intimate relatives.
- People in Authority.
- Colleagues.
- Subordinates.
- Salesperson – garage mechanics.

Situations

Note any problems you experience in the following situations:

- Home.
- Work.
- Social life – pub, parties, clubs, hobbies.
- Consultations with professionals – doctors, solicitors, etc.
- Neighbours.
- Extended family.
- Church, political parties, etc.

Personal Problem Hierarchy

Use the completed Personal Problem Profile to list your problems in order of their importance.

For example:

1. My relationship with my husband.
2. My inability to cope with my sister's bossiness.
3. Saying 'NO' to extra hours at work.
4. Criticizing colleagues.
5. Using put-down and patronizing language to my children.
6. Saying 'NO' to request for help at jumble sales, etc.
7. Asking the doctor for more information.
8. Asking my neighbour to turn down his hi-fi.
9. Sending cold food back in a restaurant.
10. Giving my friends compliments.

Setting Goals

What is a man's first duty? The answer's brief — to be himself.

Ibsen

In Assertiveness Training, resolutions are not just for the New Year. They become part of our daily life. This may, at first, sound rather heavy and awesome but it certainly should not feel so with practice.

The secret to successful goal setting is to make sure that your objectives are realistic. Most unassertive people continually set themselves up for failure. They make impossible demands on their time and energy, and then castigate themselves for their lack of achievement.

It is not uncommon for example, for chronically shy people attending Assertiveness Training sessions in their early stages to recount disastrous tales of trips to large parties and busy discotheques. They are often desperate to prove to themselves and others that they are really trying, so armed with some sketchy assertiveness theory they throw themselves in at the deep-end. Fortunately,

Assertiveness Training groups are not punitive and would not castigate them for their failure. The task of the group would be to help them to be more aware of their self-destructive behaviour and set more realistic goals.

When an attempt to meet these goals has been made, the group would then be ready and willing to offer rewards. The rewards in this situation would simply be praise and encouragement from people who truly understand and appreciate the achievement.

When we are planning our own Assertiveness Training programme, rewards are equally important. It can help if you make a list of your simple everyday pleasures, such as:

- Listening to music.

- Hot bath.

- Drink with friends.

- Chocolate cake.

- Walk through the park.

- New book or clothes.

You can then vow to treat yourself with one of these pleasures as soon as you have achieved one of your goals.

For example, 'If I ring up my mother and tell her that I have changed my mind about the arrangements for Saturday – I will reward myself by sitting down for half an hour and listening to a favourite record.'

> *The greatest thing in the world is to know how to be self-sufficient.* Michel de Montaigne

Chapter 3
Knowing Your Rights

There is no duty we so much under-rate as being happy.
R.L. Stevenson

An acceptance that we have a right to assert our needs, wants and feelings with other people is of fundamental importance. The definition of assertive behaviour quoted in Chapter 1 makes reference to basic human rights and I will now clarify what I mean by these rights. I should emphasize that this is simply the definition of rights which I have found from experience helps people who are trying to become more assertive.

Rights are anything which we think human beings are entitled to by virtue of their very existence.
In relationships, rights may also be described as reasonable expectations by one person of another.

Although each individual is ultimately responsible for his own values, the following list covers some of the most important Basic Human Rights the assertive person aims to respect for both himself and others:

Assertive Rights
1. The right to ask for what we want (realizing that the other person has the right to say 'No').

2. The right to have an opinion, feelings and emotions and to express them appropriately.
3. The right to make statements which have no logical basis, and which we do not have to justify (e.g. intuitive ideas and comments).
4. The right to make our own decisions and to cope with the consequences.
5. The right to choose whether or not to get involved in the problems of someone else.
6. The right not to know about something and not to understand.
7. The right to make mistakes.
8. The right to be successful.
9. The right to change our mind.
10. The right to privacy.
11. The right to be alone and independent.
12. The right to change ourselves and be assertive people.

Many people coming to Assertiveness Training groups have little difficulty in accepting these rights for others but their life-style and behaviour indicate that they do not accept them for themselves. They are often over-tolerant of other people's mistakes and quick to make excuses for them:

'She's only young . . .'

'He didn't realize what he was doing . . .'

'It probably will not happen again anyway.'

On the other hand, when they make mistakes themselves, it is a different story. You may hear:

'I should have known better.'

'I'm useless, I never get it right.'

This kind of negative self-talk has to stop, and in order to do this we may need the help of our family, friends or Assertiveness Training group. We are often unaware that we are abusing our own rights and it is helpful to ask people to let you know when they hear or see you doing so.

Here are some simple examples taken from Assertiveness Training groups of how some people have been abusing their own rights:

'I get a taxi to work but I make it stop round the corner from the office so no-one will see'

(Right No. 8)

'I felt I had to complete the course even though I knew it was useless to me'

(Rights Nos. 7 & 9)

'I often have great ideas but cannot always understand why they should work . . . I don't say anything even though I know they will work'

(Rights Nos. 6 & 3)

'I never seem to have a moment to myself – there is always someone in the house'

(Right No. 10)

'We always go on holiday together even though we know we need to get away from each other sometimes'

(Right No. 11)

The last statement is an example of how the abuse of certain rights can become a habit within a whole family. This, of course, makes it all the more difficult for an individual to begin to assert himself but we must remember that **an assertive person is not just concerned about his own rights but always encourages and promotes assertiveness in others**. And if our efforts at producing assertive behaviour in others fail, we cannot take responsibility for their hurt or discomfort, or let it prevent us from asserting our own rights.

If, after having completed the suggested exercises on rights and confidence building, you are still finding it difficult to accept these basic humanistic principles, it would be worth exploring the problem in more detail. It may be that you have acquired a strong counter-belief in your early childhood or that there is someone very influential in your life who does not wish you to exert your rights. If this is the case, I would advise some additional therapy such as counselling or self-help group. Unless you accept your **right** to be assertive you may find it difficult to develop any useful skills.

Assertiveness Training is not a cure-all but it can help us to be true to ourselves.

Chapter 4
The Art of Being Positive

He who desires but acts not, breeds pestilence. Bacon

Being assertive is not just a way of coping with negative and problematic situations. It is also about taking positive and constructive steps forward. It involves initiating and nurturing the kind of lifestyle and relationships we want for ourselves.

The assertive person will not sit back and trust to luck. He will actively seek out what he wants – for example a job that suits him, hobbies that interest him and friends who stimulate and support him. In seeking to find what he wants, his self-confidence will allow him to take risks and make some mistakes. What sort of risks these are will, of course, vary from person to person and each individual must be responsible for deciding which chances he wishes to take.

Most unassertive people have experienced years of 'playing it safe' and often they have been motivated to come to an Assertiveness Training class because they are bored. They are bored with their work, their family, their social life and often the predictability of their own behaviour. They may not be experiencing any major problems in their life but neither are they having much fun and excitement.

> *He that is afraid to shake the dice will never throw a six.*
> Chinese Proverb

Giving Compliments

A relatively safe, though not necessarily very easy, way of starting to take risks is to start by practising the art of compliment sharing.

The main risk, of course, involved with giving a compliment is that it will be rejected. Unfortunately this happens all too frequently in our society. The following examples will ring bells for most of us:

> 'Oh, I like your dress Mary, it really suits you.'
> *Reply*:   'Oh! I've had it ages.'
> 'I met your boy today at school – he's a great lad.'
> *Reply*:   'Oh! but he's a terror at home sometimes.'

If we sincerely want to improve our ability to compliment other people, we must practise taking compliments in an assertive, graceful manner from other people. We must learn not to dismiss them but to try to smile and say 'thank-you'. If we honestly disagree with the compliment we can, of course, still choose to put our own view across, while remembering the other person still has a right to think we are wonderful!

Having learned to accept compliments and become aware of how good they are for us, we can then move on to practise giving them to other people. We should so so with a firm, clear, confident voice and preferably looking directly at the other person. There can be no better way to nurture friendship, love and respect in our relationships. We need not wait for special occasion days or buy fancy cards to tell

our friends and family how much we appreciate them. A very common pre-occupation with people who are bereaved are thoughts such as:

'Why didn't I tell her how much she meant to me . . . I'd love to have her back for just five minutes to tell her what a wonderful mother she was.'

In therapy sessions, I often use psychodrama techniques to help people say the kind of things they would have liked to have said to their loved ones before they died. In an ideal world perhaps when everyone is superbly assertive, my therapeutic skills should be redundant!

Improving Our Self-Esteem

Tho' modesty be a virtue, bashfulness is a vice. Proverb

A good reason for not asserting yourself is, of course, that you think you are not worth the effort!

Most people who come to Assertiveness Training courses have this belief lurking somewhere around in the background. Some have it very much in the foreground and know only too well how their poor image of themselves is fundamental to their problems.

The reality of modern day life is such that everyone is beset with situations which can be potentially damaging to their self-esteem. We live in a complex competitive society and are constantly bombarded with media images of how we ought to look, behave and feel. I know that just trying on a new dress under the scornful watch of impeccably dressed sales-girls and fellow customers can temporarily knock the stuffing out of my self-esteem!

Most of us can benefit from giving our self-esteem an occasional boost. It is especially important to be feeling confident and good about yourself before embarking on some of the more threatening and risky exercises in an Assertiveness Training programme.

Humility is only doubt. Blake

Perhaps it is particularly difficult for the British to embark upon a confidence building programme. In our culture we tend to be bashful about our talents and skills. Humility is considered a virtue and certainly bragging is regarded as sinful. So you can, therefore, expect to feel a bit silly and embarrassed and 'naughty' when first attempting the exercises. Try to cope with these feelings because you will certainly find that they will help to strengthen your self-esteem.

In Assertiveness Training we usually find it helpful to exaggerate the kind of behaviour we are seeking to learn. When you return to the 'real world', your anxiety will naturally lead you to tone down your approach, so you have no need to fear appearing big-headed or egocentric!

You should feel free to boast to your heart's content in an Assertiveness Training group and in return you should receive nothing but praise!

Most therapists I know are in agreement that low self-esteem is at the heart of almost every mental health problem, whatever the symptom. Having a basically bad opinion of yourself makes you vulnerable to any kind of stress or set-back and it makes you resistant to all kinds of love and support from other people. For example, when I am doing training sessions with successful professional people, they have no difficulty in making a realistic evaluation of their professional worth, but often they cannot value their achievements in their personal life. In other groups the problem may be reversed.

Our image of ourselves depends, of course, very much on how we were valued as children. For example, our academic achievements may have been more highly regarded than our attempts to cook a meal or help look after a baby brother. As adults, we must learn to stand by our own values and judge ourselves by our own standards. Ultimately, our opinion of ourselves is the only one that matters. Do we even truly accept a compliment unless we agree with it?

Don't hide your light under a bushel. Proverb

New Horizons

Another way gently to increase our ability to take risks is to give ourselves the chance of new experiences. For example, you can make a contract with yourself or your group that each week you will try to do something different, to give yourself a new experience.

For example, when I first started Assertiveness Training I set myself the task of visiting a youth club. I had become aware that in the course of my everyday life, I had very little contact with teenagers. I was beginning to develop some horrible stereo-typed images and prejudices about them. I found myself making assumptions: they were arrogant, precocious, and cynical and suspicious of middle-aged ladies like me!

I chose to spend an evening at an Inner City Youth Club and was quaking in my shoes throughout the journey there. Needless to say, my prejudices were unconfirmed and I found a very mixed group of **individuals**, some of whom I could relate to and others with whom I had very little in common.

This experience made me realize how much I feared being rejected as being stuffy and old-fashioned. My prejudices had more to do with this fear than with teenage behaviour itself. The fact that I was accepted by the group as more or less part of the furniture did wonders for my self-esteem.

Examples of risks other people have chosen to take to expand their horizons are:

- Starting up a conversation with someone in a bus queue.
- Going to a discotheque.
- Girl going into a pub alone.
- Seeing a film they would not normally have chosen.
- A change of hair colour.
- Buying a sweater from a different kind of shop.
- Starting to play a musical instrument.

- Taking up an evening class in a new subject.

Once again it is important to respect the golden rule of Assertiveness Training. Start with a 'mini-risk' and **gradually** work towards taking the big chances with your life.

Good Communication

An assertive person is not necessarily highly articulate or a brilliant public speaker but he can:

- Listen well.
- Speak concisely.
- Initiate and maintain conversations.
- Disclose his own thoughts and feelings with ease.
- Be aware of non-verbal communication.
- Have an ability to be calm and relaxed.

All these are areas which can be effectively worked on in an Assertiveness Training group. I have included a number of exercises in Part II which I have found useful, but not all of them need to be completed by each group. How hard you will need to work on these skills is something you will have to assess for yourselves. The exercises can be fun and a good 'warm-up' for the latter part of the programme. Remember that people's ability to communicate effectively within personal relationships sometimes has little to do with their intelligence or academic achievements. We sometimes under-rate the importance of being able to make small talk, which is often the way most social relationships begin.

> *When two Englishmen meet their first talk is of the weather.*
> Samuel Johnson

Personal Appearance

Assertive people are not only confident in their behaviour but also in their personal appearance.

> *It is only shallow people who do not judge by appearances.*
> Isaak Walton

In my groups, I often do exercises which help people to become more aware of their appearance. It is good to stop and think consciously why you are wearing your particular clothes or hair-style. Disclosing to someone else what kind of impression you were trying to make is an uncomfortable exercise but it is very useful if you can get some helpful feedback.

It is very common for people who have completed an Assertiveness Training programme to change their appearance in some way. As they become more confident they are able to wear what suits them. This may mean a change to more outrageous eye-catching clothes, or alternatively adopting a very casual relaxed appearance. It may also mean wearing make-up or shaving off a beard. **Whatever the style, it is important that it truly reflects you and your mood**.

> *Liberty consists in doing what one desires.* Proverb

Chapter 5

Fundamental Assertive Skills

The best things are hard to come by.   Proverb

Persistence

Most unassertive people take 'no' for an answer far too easily. There is a growing awareness in our society that this tendency is jeopardizing the rights of large numbers of people. For example, in recent years there has been an upsurge in consumer protection organizations and pressure groups. This is a welcome development as there will always be a need for such organizations to protect the interests of individuals and minorities in a competitive society. The danger is that we can become over-dependent on professional workers for our rights and lose the art of asserting ourselves. It is better for your self-esteem and relationships with other people if you can learn the art of persistence for yourself.

We have to learn to ignore some of the not-so-pleasant messages that may be ringing in our unconscious minds, such as:

'If you ask once more – I'll flatten you.'

'You're a nagger – just like your mother.'
'Don't make a scene.'
'Anything to keep the peace.'

The main technique that we use in Assertiveness Training to practise the art of persistence is called **Broken Record**. When a record is scratched we hear one sentence over and over again until we reach screaming pitch and jump up to turn it off.

BROKEN RECORD is the skill of being able to:

repeat over and over again, in an assertive and relaxed manner, what it is you want or need, until the other person gives in or agrees to negotiate with you.

This technique is extremely useful for:

● dealing with situations where your rights are clearly in danger of being abused.

● coping with situations where you are likely to be diverted by clever, articulate but irrelevant arguments.

● situations where you are likely to lose your self-confidence because you know you could be affected by 'digs' and 'put-downs' to your self-esteem.

The beauty of using **broken record** is that once you have prepared your lines, you can relax. You have nothing more to worry about because you know exactly what you are going to say, however abusive or manipulative the other person tries to be.

As with most Assertive techniques, it must be used appropriately. It is a **self-protective skill** and is not designed to foster deep interesting conversations and friendships with people! It is primarily useful in situations where your time and energy is precious.

For example:

- when a persuasive colleague rings you at tea time and you do not want to spend hours explaining **why** you cannot help with the jumble sale.
- it's your only free shopping day in the month and you want your money back on unsatisfactory goods so that you can quickly replace them elsewhere.

Energy is eternal delight. Blake

When you have mastered the first Broken Record exercise, you can then move on to practising a more sophisticated variant. You practise conveying the same message but using slightly different words each time.

The question that I am constantly asked is, 'What happens when two assertive people meet and practise Broken Record?'

My experience is that each person quickly realizes what is happening and neither will want to continue for long. Assertive people will respect assertive behaviour when they meet it and will be ready to **negotiate**. If compromise is not acceptable you may decide to take further action or at the very least give vent to your feelings (e.g. justifiable anger) about the situation. In such cases, **do not forget to reward yourself** for your courageous effort, because it can so easily be overshadowed by the disappointment of not getting what you want.

If at first you don't succeed try, try again. Proverb

Negotiation

The art of negotiation like so many other assertive skills, is becoming a profession in its own right. We certainly do not need a sophisticated training in diplomacy to negotiate solutions to ordinary everyday problems, but a little tact and forethought will certainly help.

● Empathize	:	with the other person, i.e. really try to understand what it feels like to be in his shoes. If the other person is showing any feeling, acknowledge that you are aware of it.
Say – for example	:	'I can see this is an important issue for you'
		'I can see that you are busy . . .'
		'I understand that you don't like doing the washing up,'
● Ask for clarification	:	make sure that you fully understand their position, their reasoning and their needs.
● Keep calm	:	if possible use relaxation techniques to help you prepare for a situation you know will be tricky. At the very least, take a couple of long, slow, deep breaths before you start.
● Be prepared	:	do your homework thoroughly and get together any facts and figures that may support your case.
● Keep to the point	:	beware of becoming side-tracked and don't fall for red herrings. Ensure that the other party always keeps to the point as well. Sometimes BROKEN

		RECORD is a useful technique to use to bring the discussion back to the central subject.
● Offer a compromise	:	don't be stubborn and wait for the other person to 'give in' first.

Chapter 6

Self-Protective Skills

Coping with 'Put-Downs'

'Put-down' is a term frequently used in Assertiveness Training. A 'put-down' is **a question or remark from another person which violates one or more of your Basic Human Rights**.

These are remarks and questions designed to make you feel small or manipulate you into doing or saying something you do not wish to do or say. Sometimes the other person is quite blatant in his intentions but often they are subtly disguised and wrapped in social niceties or jokey behaviour.

For example:

'You look beautiful when you are angry'
'You're too young to understand . . .'
'I know I can always rely on you . . .'
'Come on, it's only a bit of fun . . .'

Most people come to my Assertiveness Training classes because they are justifiably fed-up with being 'put-down' by other people. Many, if they are honest, admit that they come because they want revenge – they want to learn how to be equally horrible back to the other person!

Others are only too aware of their aggressive responses to put-downs and want to know how to control them. Whether you indulge your aggressive feelings in endless circular arguments or slanging matches, or you turn them inwards and become depressed, you will certainly be using up a good deal of precious energy. This energy could be much better spent in asserting your own needs or in taking some positive action to get what you want.

Once again – the golden rule is to start with the least difficult problems. Practise coping with the 'put-downs' you get from people who matter very little to you – people with whom you are not likely to develop a close personal or working relationship. You can meet several such people in the course of one day. You may realize what is happening but talk yourself out of taking any action by thinking '. . . anyway, they're not important to me'.

There are very few people, however, whose self-esteem and energy are not affected by this kind of behaviour. Sometimes these little incidents can build up into enormous feelings of frustration which may get taken out on other people (or pets!), who have done very little to deserve the anger.

Luckily my own children can now recognize when my irritable behaviour with them is ill-deserved. My eleven year old daughter will pull me to attention by saying:

'Come on, Mum, just because you've had a bad day at work, there's no need to take it out on us; I only asked . . .'

Other children may not be so assertive and may turn their 'It's not fair' feeling inwards. If that kind of interaction happened regularly their self-esteem would suffer and they could well become seriously depressed or find an outlet in angry rebellious behaviour.

As I said earlier, 'put-downs' come in all sorts of disguises and our first task is to learn to quickly recognize them in both our own and others' behaviour.

Here are some examples which I have adapted from

Sharon Bower and Gordon Bower's *Asserting Yourself: A Practical Guide for Positive Change*. They will probably start some bells ringing!

The nasty 'hidden message' is in the brackets and is followed by a suggested assertive response.

Nagging:
'Haven't you finished the washing up yet?'
('You are useless')
'No, when did you want it done?'

Prying:
'I know I shouldn't really be nosey but . . .'
('I can easily get round you – you'll tell me anything')
'Well, I won't tell you if I don't want to . . .'

Lecturing:
'We should co-operate and then there would be less tension.'
('I'm OK – you should fall in line with me. It's your fault')
'How could we co-operate?'

Putting on the Spot:
'Are you busy on Wednesday?'
('Ha! Ha! I'll get you to agree to do something you don't want to do. I've got you on the spot if you say you are free')
'What did you have in mind?'

Questioning Choice:
'Are you sure this job is the right one for you?'
('You are not capable of choosing a job for yourself')
'It feels OK for me at the moment . . .'

Unwanted Advice:
'If I were you . . .'
('I know better than you . . .')
'But you are not!'

Insulting Labels:

'That's a typical woman's reaction . . .'
('You're just a stereotype – not an individual')
'It's my reaction and it's up to me to judge my own behaviour.'

Amateur Psychologist:

'You'll find it difficult won't you because you are so shy . . .'
('You're a hopeless case')
'In what ways do you think I am too shy?'

The exercises in Part II on page 97 will help you to distinguish the Assertive, Aggressive and Passive responses to these kinds of remarks and questions. When replying to 'put-downs' it is important to remember that you are simply aiming to:

1. Protect your rights and self-esteem.
2. Let the other person know you recognize the hidden message.
3. Put a **quick** stop to the put-down behaviour.

If 'put-downs' occur regularly in a close relationship, it may help to tackle the problem in the first instance in more or less the same way. The difference is that you will want a better understanding of why it is happening and understandably want to re-negotiate a better relationship.

On your part this will involve:

- Persistence

- an ability to ask for constructive criticism

- A willingness to compromise or change

When you have completed your initial Assertiveness Training course, you will be better prepared in all these areas.

In the meantime, be aware of what is happening in your close relationships but postpone dealing with the problems until you have mastered being assertive with other people.

Coping with Cricitism

This is perhaps the most dreaded part of any Assertiveness Training programme! Very few people are truly invulnerable to criticism and most of us would admit to one of the following:

- avoiding criticism – through passive or ingratiating behaviour. Sometimes it is politic to keep quiet or to stay in people's good books but an over-reliance on this kind of behaviour not only leads to boredom but attracts criticism behind people's backs or a stultifying atmosphere between them. It is not uncommon for unassertive people to complain 'I just don't know what I am doing wrong'.

- taking unfair criticism to heart – if your self-confidence is a little rocky it is very easy to absorb unfair criticism and act on it even though you may secretly disagree with your critic. Such behaviour leads to further damage to our self-confidence and a build-up of hidden anger and resentment.

- reacting aggressively to criticism – we are often tempted when receiving criticism to immediately retaliate with counter attack. This kind of reaction can, and usually does, just develop into a destructive slanging match and is certainly not the most effective way of resolving differences, though it can be a very useful way of letting off steam within a secure personal relationship. Sometimes the damage done by these kinds of exchanges can be devastating and irreparable. On reflection we might say . . . 'I don't know why I said that to him, because I didn't really mean it . . .' The most likely reason for saying 'things' we do not mean is that we are feeling threatened and usually as a result of direct or indirect criticism.

Assertive people are not frightened of criticism because they are well prepared for it and know that it can be useful to all parties concerned.

Self-Criticism

Having built up our confidence in the earlier part of the Assertiveness Training programme, the best and perhaps safest place to start confronting criticism is within ourselves. If we are aware of our own faults and are either prepared to tolerate them or take active steps to correct them, criticism from others is much easier to bear and we will be more able to give fair criticism to others.

Developing an awareness of our own faults is not easy:

You can see a mote in another's eye but cannot see a beam in your own. Proverb

But doing the simple exercises in Chapter 13 with the help of a supportive friend or a group is a good first step.

And remember:

He that is ill to himself will be no good to nobody.
Proverb

Giving Criticism to Others

Here are some hints on giving helpful and constructive criticism:

Be specific – the golden rule when giving criticism to others is to avoid generalizations. For example, it is much more useful to say . . .
'I don't think dull colours suit you' than to say
'You've go no dress sense', and to say
'You've over-spent your budget three times this year', rather than
'You're a hopeless manager'

Acknowledge the positive – if you can include some genuine positive comment do so. For example, 'You have lovely hair but I do prefer your natural colour'. However, beware of smothering your criticism with polite niceties!

As with most other assertive exchanges it helps to **empathize** with the other person's feelings or situation. For example, 'I realize what I am going to say might be disappointing to you but I do prefer . . .'

Keep calm. If you have a tendency to be aggressive or get stage fright, practise some quiet relaxation techniques before entering the situation. Keep your voice level and avoid threatening gestures.

Keep to the point – don't be tempted to bring in all your other complaints to cloud the issue and don't allow yourself to get sidetracked. 'Broken Record' could help you get back on to the point.

Focus on behaviour – don't attack the whole person, merely their behaviour or one particular aspect of their appearance. For example, say
'You always leave the bathroom in a mess', not
'You are the most untidy person I have ever known.'

Don't use labels or stereotypes – for example 'typical woman', 'You're so childish', 'Fascist pig', etc.

Finally, don't despair or feel daunted by the above. Your ability to criticize can certainly be improved with practice.

Don't be tempted to skip the exercises in Chapter 13.

Receiving Criticism

In Assertiveness Training we use three main techniques for helping us to deal with criticism from others. These are introduced by Manuel J. Smith in his book *When I say No, I feel Guilty.*

They are **Negative Assertion, Fogging** and **Negative Enquiry.**

In my own courses, although I have found the rehearsal of these techniques very useful, I also find that participants are often confused by the differences between them and can waste precious energy worrying about whether they have got them exactly right.

'. . . *Can waste precious energy worrying about whether they have "got it exactly right".'*

For the purpose of learning the new skill it is helpful to teach these techniques independently but remember that in practice they are likely to be incorporated into a whole pattern of assertive behaviour. All that matters is that you understand and accept the basic principle, and that you can discern the difference between helpful criticism and 'put-down' behaviour.

Negative Assertion

If you have completed your self-criticism exercises honestly and thoroughly, this technique should be relatively easy!

Negative assertion is calmly agreeing with the true criticism of your negative qualities. For example:

*'This desk is a complete and utter tip . . .
you're hopelessly disorganized!'*

You can reply,

'Yes it is true I am not very tidy.'

'. . . *It may be because they have not yet learned to accept that fault in themselves.'*

When I introduce this technique, people often say, '. . . but surely you are just putting yourself down and opening up the channels for further criticisms.'

In my experience, if you are genuinely happy to accept that you have faults, and that you are not perfect, people will be less likely to put you down. Not many people are comfortable with 'goody-gum-drops'. They are too aware of their own imperfections! The key to learning to use Negative Assertion is, of course, self-confidence together with the conviction that you have an ability to change and improve yourself if you so wish. It may help to remind yourself of the ironic truth that if a particular fault of yours intensely annoys someone, it may be because they have not yet learned to accept that fault in themselves!

I get furious when I see my husband scratching his knees or elbows and I know that my fury is really with myself because I still have not learnt to control my own scratching habits!

Mutual forgiveness of each vice
Such are the gates of Paradise. Bacon

Fogging

If you deal with a fox, think of his tricks. Proverb

This is a skill which helps us to cope with manipulative criticism. This kind of criticism is eventually a 'put-down' and designed to make you feel bad about yourself or make you do something you do not want to do. There is often an element of truth in what is being said but the critic may elaborate or exaggerate.

For example

'You're late this morning . . . you're always late . . . you don't care about anyone else here . . . you expect us to do all your dirty work . . .'

In all probability the only real truth in the accusation is:

'You're late . . .'

but nevertheless the onslaught succeeds in leaving you feeling so guilty that you meekly agree to doing hours of unpaid overtime.

The technique of **fogging** is to calmly acknowledge that there may be some truth in what is being said.

Fogging can be used on its own or, perhaps more usefully, it can be used together with a sentence which reflects your assessment of the situation:

For example, in reply to the above statement you may say,

'Yes I am late this morning. It is possible that I am not as committed to work as I could be.'

Another example would be:

'You look terrible this morning. Those clothes look as though they have never seen a washing machine and your hair . . .'

You could reply:

'You are probably right, I don't look my best this morning.'

By using the technique of **fogging** you are merely aiming to stop the manipulative criticism and protect your self-esteem. You achieve this by refusing to reward the put-down behaviour. Your attacker, after all, wants you to feel hurt and upset. If he does not get what he wants he is less likely to try again.

When using **fogging** always remember that whatever the other person says or thinks you have the right to be the judge of your own behaviour and you also have the right to defend this right!

Patience under old injuries invites new ones. Proverb

Negative Enquiry

This is perhaps the most difficult of all the techniques to use but is very useful in improving communication particularly in personal relationships.

Negative Enquiry involves you in: actively prompting criticism of your behaviour.

I used an example of this technique in my earlier chapter on 'put-downs':

'You'll find that difficult won't you because you are so shy?'

The assertive responsive using Negative Enquiry was:

'In what ways do you think I am too shy?'

This kind of reply will very quickly help you decide if your critic is genuinely concerned about your shyness or merely wants to put you down. The 'nasty' character will probably be thrown by your response and may just continue to put you down and refuse to be specific.

For example, *'Goodness, what a question. You wouldn't really want to know . . . I'm not a psychiatrist you know . . .'*

Once you have exposed your critic's real intentions you can deal with any further put-downs by Fogging them and asserting your right to be the judge of your own behaviour.

If, however, your critic is genuinely concerned about you he might respond to your assertive reply by saying:

'. . . well, I've noticed that you always wait for other people to start conversations and you never look people straight in the eye.'

He may even add a compliment:

'. . . I have noticed though, that you have been really trying lately.'

This latter criticism is constructive and could be very useful feedback.

When first practising Negative Enquiry, it is important to choose people whom you trust and whose opinion you respect.

> *A man cannot be too careful about his choice of enemies.*
>
> Proverb

If you start by inviting criticism from other people you obviously run a much higher risk of getting 'put-down' or hearing superficial feedback. Neither experience will enhance your self-esteem and both are best avoided. When your confidence has improved, feedback from acquaintances can be very useful especially in situations when you experience difficulty in asserting yourself.

For example, I know someone who has recently done some Assertiveness Training and is actively trying to get a

'Beware of smothering your criticism with polite niceties!'

job after many years of unemployment. He was convinced, maybe quite rightly, that his presentation at his last interview prevented him from getting the job, which was well within his capabilities. He had the courage to use Negative Enquiry with his interviewers and received some useful feedback – not all of which was negative. The firm was obviously impressed by his assertiveness and put him on the waiting list.

The exercises in Chapter 6 are designed to give you a chance to practise taking criticism. If anyone has difficulty in doing the exercises, try 'going over the top'. Exaggerate and 'ham-up' your performances. This makes the scenario less life-like and introduces some fun. It will still be a very useful exercise and it is certainly better than avoiding this area altogether.

It is often a good idea to round-off these criticism sessions with some genuine positive feedback. You can counteract the gloom and despair with a little compliment sharing or boasting!

Chapter 7
Getting Prepared

> *Knowledge without practice makes but half the artist.*
>
> **Proverb**

To the untrained eye, assertive people often appear to be very spontaneous and direct in their approach to problems. Although this behaviour may seem very natural and off the cuff, it is often the result of very thorough preparation and rehearsal.

Before tackling a tricky situation an assertive person will think objectively through all the aspects of the problem and will be aware of the feelings of all the parties involved. He may even have thought out and rehearsed in some detail, a plan of action.

The **two main tools** we use in Assertiveness Training to help us to prepare for potentially difficult situations are:

Scripting – the written preparation of an 'opening speech' or letter.
Role Play – the acting out of problematic situations and the rehearsal of appropriate assertive behaviour.

Both techniques are best used with real-life situations. For training purposes, you can take either an unsatisfactory experience from the past, a current problem or an anticipated situation.

Whether you choose to use Scripting or Role Play will depend on many factors, such as the following:

Situation – some problems are best tackled in written form. Remember that an assertive letter may be a good starting point especially for anyone who is terrified by the thought of a face-to-face encounter!

Size of the group – for an effective role-play you obviously need all the main characters in the scenario plus some observers. Scripting can be done by yourself although discussion with other people is certainly helpful.

Individual preference – some people seem to think better when they are using pen and paper whilst others find action more useful.

Time available – a role-play can be a lengthy experience, whereas with practice scripting can be done very much more quickly.

Non-verbal communication – and its relative importance. Some people have little difficulty in finding the right assertive words but are not able to match these with the appropriate assertive voice, eye contact etc. Role play would be an obvious choice with such a problem.

Both Scripting and Role-Play are very effective although I feel that a Role-Play done within a supportive group leaves a bigger impression and often has the added advantage of being fun as well. In my groups, I now usually use Scripting exercises as a 'warm up' for role-play sessions.

Scripting

Sharon Bower, an American counsellor and co-author of the book *Asserting Yourself* introduced the idea of 'scripting' into her Assertiveness Training sessions during the 1970's. She used her earlier professional experience in the theatre to develop a new way of helping people prepare themselves for interpersonal conflicts. In my own training programmes, I have used many of her ideas and have recently formulated another model of scripting which seems to be very effective.

The basic idea of scripting is that you can take a situation that is causing problems and view it as you would a scene from a play. It involves looking at the setting and the characters – taking into account their feelings, motivation and behaviour. Having done this you can rewrite the 'script' so that *you* are the character with the powerful opening speech. This will give you more of a chance to influence the proceedings and hopefully produce an ending which is fairer and more reasonable for all the characters involved. The new 'play' may not make such good drama for an audience but hopefully it will improve the relationships of the participating characters!

There are several ways of preparing your new script. You can write it down, word for word, or you can prepare a rough outline and leave room for improvisation.

There are four main components to think about when preparing your script. The following sentence should help you to remember them.

Even	Fish	Need	Confidence
X	E	E	O
P	E	E	N
L	L	D	S
A	I	S	E
N	N		Q
A	G		U
T	S		E
I			N
O			C
N			E
			S

Explanation

- Explain the situation as *you* see it.

- Be as *objective* as possible.

- Keep to the *point* – don't be tempted to bring in other issues and past experiences.

- Be *brief* – to avoid the other person 'switching off' or 'butting in'.

- *Don't theorize* – stick to describing what has happened or is happening and *not why* you think it is happening.

Feelings

Acknowledge your own feelings and own them as your responsibility. Don't accuse the other person of making you feel anything. For example, say 'I'm angry' *not* 'You make me angry'.

Empathize with the other person's feelings or situation. Try to get into their shoes (e.g. 'I can see that you are irritated' or 'I know that you are in a difficult situation'). This shows the other person that you are thinking of him as well as of yourself and if you have correctly empathized with him, it will obviate the necessity for him to convince you of how he feels. This is a useful technique to use when someone is angry. Anger is only a way of communicating how upset you feel. Once that message is acknowledged there is less need for angry behaviour and more room for rational discussion.

When a man is angry his reason rides out. Proverb

Needs

Your next step is to outline clearly what it is that you want

69

out of the situation. You must say what you need to happen so that the situation can be resolved.

- Be selective – make as few demands as possible at any one time. Try to start with just one.

- Be realistic – make sure the other person has the power to give you what you want, e.g. don't demand a total personality change, or a revolution, unless you honestly think either is feasible.

- Be prepared to compromise – or negotiate unless it is a situation where your basic human rights are being flagrantly abused.

Invite constructive criticism of your behaviour and indicate that you may be prepared to change.

Consequences

Finally, you must outline what will happen if the other person does what you have requested:

- Outline the rewards – these may be quite simple, e.g. that you will feel thankful, happier, or less irritable, or that you will continue to shop at that greengrocers, or work harder at your job.

Or, if they do not do what you have requested:

- Outline the punishments – e.g. your relationship will deteriorate or you will withhold your custom or change your job.

Remember that it is always a good idea to try rewards before punishments, but I advise people to think out the negative consequences before they write their script. They can then realistically assess their power in the situation even if they may never need to use it.

Empty threats are worse than useless, and the 'punishment' must always fit the crime. Thorough preparation of our scripts before entering the situation helps us not to over-react or threaten the impossible.

● Remember – one of the secrets of good scripts is to keep them short and concise.

Deliver your words not by number but by weight.

Proverbs

The following are small sample scripts:

Sample Scripts

Example 1.

My neighbour's stereo has been keeping me awake until the early hours of the morning.

Explanation
'I would like to talk over a problem with you. During the past week I have had two disturbed nights because your stereo kept me awake until two o'clock in the morning'

Feelings
'I am beginning to feel tired and irritated and although I can appreciate how important listening to music is to you . . .'

Needs
'. . . if you would turn the volume down after midnight

Consequences
'. . . I'd be very grateful.'

71

Example 2.

I am a Nurse Tutor and I am having difficulty in confronting a student with his failure to complete his written assessments.

Explanation
'Now then, I would like to talk about your assessments. You are nearing the end of your training and you haven't attempted any assessments yet.'

Feelings
'I know you have had problems, but I'm worried in case you don't have time to do these before your finals.'

Needs
'I would like you to attempt one during the next month.'

Consequences
'By doing so, you will have more time for study before your final exam.'

Role Play

A great part of courage is having done the thing before.
Emerson

The first point to remember when considering role play is that it has very little to do with drama and acting! Many people say 'I couldn't possibly do it. I was never any good at acting.'

Remember – you do not need to be an actor to do role play! You are not preparing a performance but rehearsing behaviour for real life situations! In my experience, role play is the most effective method of acquiring assertive skills so please do try to combat the initial embarrassment and test it out.

Role play is not to be confused with 'Psychodrama' which is a very powerful form of therapy which aims to resolve unconscious conflicts within the personality. Although Psychodrama also consists of the 'acting out' of problematic situations, these are directed by experienced therapists and tend to explore feelings rather than behaviour. Important traumatic incidents and relationships are often 're-lived' in order to achieve the emotional release and new insight.

As I have had some training and experience in Psychodrama, I have poached a few of its techniques for use in Assertiveness Training role-plays, but we must always be aware of the difference between the two therapies. I have developed the following model for role-play which can be used by self-help groups. The word **protagonist** is used to describe the person presenting the problem and the word **auxilliary** to describe the other participants in the scene.

Nine Stages in a Role Play

1) Initial Discussion:
The main task here is to choose a 'scene' to role play. For your first effort, spend some time selecting one which will be of interest to the majority of the group. Sometimes it is tempting to rush in to do the first one that is volunteered!

Have your Personal Problem Profiles handy and use them to refresh your memory. It is amazing how quickly we can forget our problems at the suggestion of a role play session!

Alternatively, break up into pairs or small groups and discuss certain problem areas, for example

- Difficulty in saying 'No'
- Complaining

- Asking for money
- Standing up to your parents, etc.

After ten minutes or so, a number of 'scenes' are likely to emerge which would be suitable to act out.

Remember – be realistic in your choice.

Do not start with a very complex relationship problem or a situation where assertive behaviour is not appropriate.

Having chosen the protagonist, you will need someone to direct the role play. The director may be your usual group leader or anyone else who feels they can help with that particular problem. Bear in mind that role play is a self-help exercise for the **whole group** and the director should not be expected to have the answers to the problem. He merely needs to *guide* the role play through its different stages.

2) Setting the Scene

The director will invite the protagonist to choose an area in the room where he would like to set the scene. The more responsibility the director gives to the protagonist for setting up the role play, the more realistic and effective it will be.

He must then define the area of the room and arrange the appropriate furniture. Imagination is sometimes aided by placing a few odd props about, e.g. cups, plates, papers, books, scarf or coat, but remember that the setting only has to feel approximately right. The director can then ask the protagonist to walk round 'the room' describing any special features, such as windows, fires, doors, television, etc.

The protagonist is then ready to choose his 'cast' or *auxiliaries*. The director should greatly encourage everyone to 'have a go' if they are asked to play a part and remind them that we can learn a good deal from being an auxiliary, whether we feel the person is very different from ourselves or very similar. As a director, beware of helping the protagonist to make his choice. I have learned to trust that protagonists have an uncanny knack of choosing the right auxiliaries for their 'play'.

Once chosen, the auxiliaries need some guidance as to how they should play their part. I have found the technique called 'egoing' in Psychodrama most useful. It consists of simply 'stepping into the other person's shoes' for a minute and describing them and their perception of the 'scene' in the first person.

For example, Kevin egoing his father:

'I am Bill, Kevin's father, I am 62. Stockily built! I am very jovial and don't like to hurt anyone. I think most problems can be coped with if you have a sense of humour. I think Kevin is too serious and gets upset too easily. I'm a storeman; it's not a bad job though I prefer staying at home. I spend most of my spare time watching football on television. My wife is the boss of this house.'

He can then add a few key words and expressions which his father may use, for example:

'Cheer up lad, it may never happen'
'Ask your mum'
'I'm not bothered'
'Do as you like'

At any time the auxiliary can ask for further tips to enable him to play the role and the rest of the group can ask questions if they are puzzled by any aspect.

3) Warm-Up
It always helps to have a warm-up to the difficult scene. A few minutes spent running through a scene from the previous week, day or hour will help everyone to relax and get into role. This also gives the director a chance to check that the role play feels realistic to the protagonist.

4) Action
The problem scene is then improvised by the protagonist

and auxiliaries. Provided that everyone has been well 'warmed-up' and briefed this stage goes surprisingly easily. Remember that it is not always necessary to play the whole scene through to its conclusion. The group only needs to see enough to get the general picture of how the protagonist handled the situation. Sometimes re-living the whole experience is harming and embarrassing and can upset the protagonist so much that he is not able to concentrate on the next important stages in the role play.

5) First Feedback

The director now asks the whole group to give feedback to the protagonist. Here are some questions he might ask:

- Was he assertive?

- How did his aggression or passivity show?

- Did you notice any key words or gestures?

- What was his tone of voice like?

- How did the auxiliaries respond to the protagonist's words and actions?

- Can anyone suggest any alternative ways of approaching the problem?

Always remember that the focus is on everyone's behaviour and the director should curb any 'interpretations' or character analysis!

Suggestions should be as specific as possible, for example:

'Look the other person in the eye'
'Don't fidget with your fingers'
'Try saying his name'
'When he brings up what happened last week, remind him that it is not relevant'

6) Modelling

'Modelling' is a term used in social psychology and learning theory. For our purposes, it simply means someone else acting out the protagonist's role to enable him to have the chance of standing back and viewing the scene objectively. After the previous discussion, hopefully the model's performance will be more assertive, but in my experience it does not seem to matter if it is not. The most helpful part of this stage seems to be having the opportunity of seeing the role from the outside. It is important to remember that the model is not telling the protagonist how to do it, but rather running through the scene as he would like to behave. Showing the protagonist an alternative way of approaching the problem helps him to be aware that he has the choice to behave differently.

7) Second Feedback

Everyone now has a chance to discuss the model's behaviour. New ideas and approaches may now emerge. The model may well have experienced similar difficulties to the protagonist and may want to share these, for example:

'I really pity you having to cope with him. He was just trying to make me feel small all the time. It was quite a struggle!'

This kind of feedback can be very reassuring to the protagonist. He can reduce the guilt he feels about not coping well with the situation and so release some valuable energy. He can use this energy to combat the challenge. Sometimes the protagonist is surprised to hear that the model found the situation difficult because his fear and anxiety were not apparent to those watching. This enables the protagonist to see that it is possible to behave assertively while still inwardly quaking in your shoes.

> *Courage is resistance to fear, mastery of fear, not absence of fear.* Mark Twain

8) Re-Run

The protagonist, armed with support and advice runs through exactly the same scene again.

9) Final Feedback

Praise and encouragement should be the order of the day at this final stage. The protagonist may well have been so anxious that he will not realize how better he has fared. Once again, detailed specific feedback will be very helpful. For example:

'You looked him straight in the eye.'
'You didn't beat about the bush.'
'You looked calm and in control.'
'I felt less threatened by you.'
'I had more respect for you.'

The changes may sometimes seem very small to the protagonist in relation to the overall problem. It sometimes helps to remind him that the only effective way of changing is through taking small steps. One role-play cannot be expected to undo a life-time's bad habits but it is certainly a very good start!

And remember,

> *To feel brave, act as if you were brave . . . and a courage fit will very likely replace the fit of fear.* William James

78

Part 2
Practical Work

A programme of Assertiveness Training exercises for self-help groups and individuals.

Chapter 8

Practical Work on Chapter 1 Arguments for Assertiveness

What is Assertiveness?

Self-Help Groups

1) Brainstorm
In the centre of a large piece of paper or blackboard write the word

Assertive

in bold capital letters. Ask the group to look at the word and say whatever other words come into their minds.

The words are then added to the sheet like this –

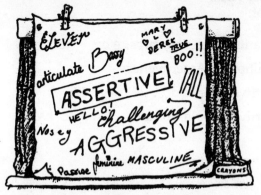

'The words are added to the sheet like this.'

The only rules are – one word at a time and do not hold back! Even the silliest of words should be put down. Continue doing the exercise until the group 'dries up'.

The leader can then start a discussion about the results of the exercise. It often helps to take two coloured felt tip pens and underline the positive and negative words. In the course of choosing which words should be classed as positive or negative, a stimulating discussion usually emerges and people become aware of each other's opinions and prejudices.

2) Definitions
Ask the group to divide into small groups of three or four people and ask each of them to come up with a definition of Assertiveness. This exercise in my experience usually produces some excellent definitions and if this happens these can be made into large posters and pinned up for the rest of the sessions. If no reasonable definition emerges make a poster of the definition on page 19.

Individuals: You can also do a Brainstorm and list the positive and negative aspects of Assertiveness. Make a poster of the definition and pin it up.

3) Visual Aids
Posters of:

- relevant quotes, proverbs, etc.

- definition of Assertiveness.

- 'assertive people do . . .' (page 19)

- 'assertive people do not . . .' (pages 19-20)

Why Are We Unassertive?

Self-Help Groups
1) Childhood Influences
Ask the group to divide into pairs and take five or ten minutes each to talk about their family and school background. They can ask each other questions such as:

● were your parents assertive?

● were you allowed to stand up for yourself?

● what were your brothers and sisters like?

● were your teachers authoritarian?

● were you bullied at school?

● have any of these experiences or relationships any bearing on your unassertiveness today?

A discussion with the whole group can now continue.

2) Key Words and Sentences
Take a large sheet of paper and some felt tip pens and ask the group to 'BRAINSTORM' any words or sentences from their past or present life which echo either consciously or unconsciously in their minds when they are unassertive, for example:

● 'be quiet!'

● 'children should be seen and not heard'

● 'that's a man's job'

● 'don't be a sissy'

● 'the meek shall inherit the Kingdom of Heaven'

● 'he is a shy child'

Remind yourself that these are merely 'old' messages and although they can be very powerful, they can be replaced. If you have time, the group can discuss each sentence in turn and decide whether it is a message you wish to continue carrying around in your head or not.

The group can then make a more acceptable list of words and pin these up as a poster.

Individuals: The above exercises can usefully be done on your own. Talk to your brothers, sisters and old school friends, and get their impressions as well. Give yourself a week or so to think about the subject and make notes as ideas come up. Pin your list of new 'Assertive' words and sentences up at home.

Why Bother to be Assertive?

Self-Help Groups

1) Let's Pretend
Each person should think of a number of assertive people they know. They then select one and think about that person, for one to five minutes, concentrating on their lifestyle, achievements, etc.

The group then walks around the room silently being their selected person. When the leader indicates, they should stop and introduce themselves, as that person, to a partner and talk about themselves for one minute each. Their partner can then introduce them to someone else in the group. The exercise can go on as long as the group is having fun!

Alternatively, you can simply find partners and talk about your selected person.

2) Guided Fantasy
The leader asks the group to lie or sit comfortably, close their eyes, and breathe slowly and deeply, and relax. He

tells them to imagine (keeping their eyes closed) that they are lying in bed and their Fairy Godmother walks in and gently waves her magic wand.

She tells them to take every advantage of this special gift. They must stay 'lying in bed' for five minutes planning how they will use these next few days.

The leader then tells everyone to find a partner and form a small group to share their fantasy.

On returning to the large group, each person can share one important part of their fantasy.

Individuals: For one week make sure you allow yourself plenty of time to day-dream! Fantasize about how different your life could be if you were assertive. Make a list of the six most important differences and pin it up in a prominent place.

Chapter 9

Practical Work on Chapter 2
The Essence of Assertiveness

Self-Help Groups
1) Walk-Around
The leader tells the group to silently think of an extremely passive person they know and then to try to 'get into their shoes' and walk around the room as though they were that person. Think of how they would use their body and exaggerate the gestures and positions. The leader then says 'Freeze' and asks everyone to look around and talk about what they observe: for example, how people are standing; holding their hands; how did they walk, etc.

The exercise is repeated for both an aggressive and an assertive person.

2) Aggression, Passivity and Assertiveness
Make three small groups and each take one of these words and list some non-verbal and verbal behaviour characteristics.

These can be compared and pinned up for reference. Alternatively, make a poster from pages 27-8 and pin that up.

Individuals: You too can try the walk-around exercise and then for the next week be as observant as you can about people's verbal and non-verbal behaviour. See how many words and phrases you can add to the chart on Pages 27-8.

Chapter 10

Practical Work on Chapter 3 Knowing Your Rights

Self-Help Groups

Make a photocopy of the list of Assertive Rights on pages 35-6 for each group member. Divide into pairs with each partner taking it in turn to read the list of rights to each other. I find it helpful to turn the list into a personal statement, so, instead of reading each right as it is written say:

'I have the right to ask for what I want (realizing that the other person has the right to say 'No').'

'I have the right to have an opinion, feelings, and emotions and express them appropriately' etc.

The person who is listening should in some way confirm that you have this right. They can do this non-verbally by, for example, nodding or smiling enthusiastically or they can reply by saying something like this:

'Yes, you have the right to have an opinion, feelings and emotions and to express them appropriately.'

You are then, in effect, giving each other some positive reinforcement which is most helpful if anyone has a difficulty in accepting and owning these rights.

After reading through the rights you can then spend

some time sharing any difficulties you may have with them. Look at the effect abusing these rights has on your life and relationships. You can then help each other select one right to work on for the following week.

Finish the exercise by each person owning the particular right they have selected with the rest of the group.

I usually suggest that people make a large poster of this right and pin it up in a conspicuous place at home or in the office. You could also try writing in your diary for each day of the week. I have found it helpful to have a reminder somewhere where you and other people supporting your efforts to change can see it.

Individuals: Read the list of rights out loud as suggested for the self-help groups. Mark the ones you feel you find it difficult to accept and make notes on how abusing these rights is stopping you getting what you want out of your life. If you are working on your own, it is very important for you to put reminder notices up for yourself. Make a goal for the next week in relation to one of the rights and note this in your diary. Share this goal with a friend or colleague and offer to support them in not abusing their rights. I have yet to meet anyone who doesn't admit to abusing at least one of these rights!

Give yourself one particular right each week to think about. Notice your own and other people's behaviour in relation to this right. Fantasize on how different your life and other people's lives would be if these rights were fully respected.

Chapter 11

Practical Work on Chapter 4
The Art of Being Positive

Giving Compliments

Self-Help Groups

From time to time in your group, you can practice giving each other compliments. Don't forget that it is often just as difficult to receive a compliment assertively as it is to give one! Although I would encourage people always to give compliments verbally if possible, a good way to start is by writing down positive comments about each other.

Here are a couple of my favourite ways of doing this:

1. Pin large sheets of paper to each person's back and then mill around in the group, writing positive comments on each other's papers.

2. At the end of a course or in a special occasion like Christmas or Easter, get or make a card for each person and encourage everyone to write positive comments on the cards. Everyone can then take these away and gloat on them from time to time!

Individuals: For a period of one week make a note in your diary of how many compliments you have given, taken or rejected each day.

The following weeks aim to give one extra compliment away each day and note how you felt and how your gesture was received.

Improving Our Self-Esteem

Self-Help Groups

Each member must answer the following questions. It helps to make a written list and then read this out to a partner in as *boastful* a manner as possible. Encourage each other to share even more achievements, etc., and then tell the rest of the group about some of these.

● Which natural feature of your body or mind do you particularly like?

● What sort of things do you do better than most people?

● What skills do you have which you are proud to have developed?

● What is the hardest thing you have accomplished in your life?

● What do you like about your personality?

● What are you most proud of in your life?

Individuals:

1. Write down the answers to the above questions and show them to a *trusted* friend. Don't ask for comment because other people's opinion of you is not relevant in this exercise. If they make a suggestion that you can add something to the list, only do so if you fully agree with them.

2. For a period of one week, make a note in your diary of all your achievements – however small they may appear

to be. Eg. – 'I listened attentively throughout a boring meeting! . . . I made Jo laugh today. I wrote a letter to my sister this week.'

Remember, you are the best judge of what is an achievement for you and be scrupulously hard with yourself.

New Horizons

Self-Help Groups

1. Divide into pairs and share with each other how easy or difficult it is for you to take risks. Make a contract with each other to take a risk during the week and agree to report back your experiences.

2. Mill around the room and every so often stop and say something to another member of the group that you have never said before.
   eg. – I like your hair.
   – I wish you would come on time for these meetings.
   – I like watching soap operas on TV.
   – I think this sweater really suits me.

Individuals:

1. Make a list of some of the goals you have in your life and then write beside them some of the risks you will need to take in order to achieve them. Examine the fears and anxieties which are maybe stopping you taking those risks and check with your list of Assertive Rights to see if you are being fair to yourself. For example, you may find that it is a fear of making mistakes which is stopping you taking a certain risk. You can then set

yourself some goals in that particular area, making sure, of course, that these are realistic and the mistakes won't be too expensive!

2. List all the new experiences you have had in the past month or year – depending on how changeable your life has been. How many of these were due to you having taken some initiative? If you can claim responsibility for only a few, make a contract with yourself to increase that number. Chart your progress over the period of a month.

Good Communication

Self-Help Groups

1. Divide into pairs. Spend three minutes each on sharing information about either yourself, an exciting holiday, a cause you believe in, or anything else you want to talk about. Each summarize, on paper, in a few sentences what both you and your partner said. Read each others summaries and discuss the differences and similarities.

2. Each member stands or sits in front of the group and talks for two minutes on any subject of their choosing. The group can then give each other feedback about the way they communicated both verbally and non-verbally. Always make sure that the feedback is constructive and specific, eg. 'Your voice was too low' *not* 'Your voice wasn't right'.

3. Mill around the room and one person take responsibility for choosing a subject matter to give people to talk about in pairs, eg. a good book; the weather; a TV programme. After a couple of minutes the group should move around and then stop, find another partner and talk on a different subject. The idea is to develop an ability to participate quickly and

spontaneously in 'small talk'. This exercise is also a very useful ice-breaker for new groups.

Individuals: It is difficult to practise the art of communicating with others on your own, but there are several ways you can try:

1. Get hold of some play scripts from the library and use these to study the communication patterns between the characters. Use the section 'Good Communication' in Chapter 4 to guide you in your assessments. As an important assertive skill is to speak concisely; you could practise summarizing the speeches made by various characters.

2. If you have access to a video, record a play and use the playback facility to study the communication. You can also stop the play at random and then practise responding spontaneously to the last few sentences which have been said. You can then compare your response to the response of the character in the play. Which was the most assertive?!

3. With the aid of a cassette player, practise talking for a minute or two on a number of 'small talk' subjects. Playback the recording and critically assess your performance.

Personal Appearance

Self-Help Groups

1. Break into pairs or small groups and each person spend a couple of minutes talking about the clothes they are wearing today. Why did they choose to wear them or buy them? Are there any stories attached to any of the items?

2. Again in pairs or small groups, ask everyone to imagine the clothes they would wear and the hairstyle they would have if they had unlimited funds and unlimited confidence!

3. One person can set up themselves in the corner of the room and pretend to run a magic shop. Members of the group can in turn go to the shop and try on and buy any item of clothing they wish. They can ask the group to help them decide whether it suits them or not! This exercise can be fun but also very revealing. Spend some time sharing with each other what has been learned and, if you want to, make a contract to change your appearance in some minor way so that it is slightly nearer the image you would like to project.

Individuals: Spend an hour or so looking through your wardrobe and assessing your hairstyle. Are you comfortable with the way you look? If not spend some time over the next few weeks being very aware of other people's appearance. Without committing yourself financially, go into a variety of shops and try on different styles of clothes. As a reward, buy yourself some minor treat and remind yourself that the only rules in this game are that your appearance should match you and your mood!

Chapter 12

Practical Work on Chapter 5 Fundamental Assertive Skills

The Art of Persistence

Self-Help Groups

Divide into small groups of three or four people and choose an appropriate situation in which to rehearse the skill of Broken Record.

Use one of your own scenes or select some from this list:

- Taking bad fruit back to the greengrocers.

- Refusing a door-to-door salesman.

- Telling children it's time for bed.

- Refusing a date from a persistent admirer.

- Saying 'no' to a request to join a committee.

- Refusing to work overtime or change shifts.

Take turns in practising the technique, firstly repeating exactly the same sentence. Secondly, try slightly altering your words but ensure that the message is exactly the same.

When you have mastered the technique, practise using it together with a sentence which empathizes with the other person. For example, 'I can appreciate that you are in a difficult position (empathy) but I would like a refund today, please'. (Broken Record).

Individuals: You can do the above exercise in written form. Don't forget to bring in all the irrevelant arguments and 'put-downs' you can think of. Rehearse saying your sentence out loud a few times before using it in a real-life situation.

Successful Negotiation

Self-Help Groups

Divide into groups of three or four and spend some time sharing some personal problems, either from the past or present, which you think could possibly be resolved by negotiation. Choose one or more of these situations and select two people to 'act-out' a negotiating scene. For the purposes of this exercise it is not necessary to do a full role-play as described in Chapter 7, but merely ensure that you have a chance to practise the skills described in this chapter.

Remember it is important to select a situation where there is room for negotiation, and group discussion can help you do this. Emotional involvement with problems can easily blind us to their potential solutions, so it is worth sharing even the most seemingly intractable ones.

Individuals: Use the technique of 'Scripting' (see Chapter 7) to help you prepare some scripts for use in negotiating. If possible, show these to a friend and ask for comment, as it is very easy to be unrealistic when doing this exercise on your own. Carefully check your script against the tips given in this chapter and make sure that you have not put yourself down in any way or made an impossible demand on the other person.

Chapter 13

Practical Work on Chapter 6 Self-Protective Skills

Coping with Put-Downs

Self-Help Groups

Break into small groups and each take one or two examples of the 'put-down' sentences given in Chapter 6 (pages 54–5). As a group, discuss the three possible responses to these sentences using the Aggressive, Passive and Assertive responses. When you have finished, share these with the rest of the group and check your results with the examples of assertive replies.

During the next few weeks, everyone should be on the look out for put-down behaviour. Start each session with sharing your 'real life' experiences and discuss ways of coping with them.

Individuals: Take the sentences on pages 54–5 and think of an assertive response to each one. Check your replies with the examples given. In the next few weeks, note down any put-down behaviour you spot towards you or others, and then think about it in relation to this chapter and work out an assertive response.

Remember!
Sometimes it is not possible to reply assertively to 'put-

downs' as soon as they are received and there should be no great shame in taking issue with the other person the next time you meet him (or her).

Coping with Criticism

Self-Help Groups
Self-Criticism
Everyone should write down one or two examples from their own life in the following areas:

- Natural handicap or imperfection
  e.g. Nose is too large.
       High-pitched voice.

- Mistakes
  e.g. 'I didn't work hard enough at school'
       'I chose the wrong job for me'
       'I married too young (or too late)'

- Faults
  e.g. 'I am untidy'
       'I don't stand up for myself'
       'I nag my children'
       'I am extravagant'

When you have completed your list, find a partner with whom you would feel happy to share it. Each person should listen in an accepting way to the faults etc., of their partner. Remember that the other person has a right not to like his own nose or his untidiness even if you find both very endearing!

Individuals: You could do the above exercise on your own or with the help of a friend, or alternatively, try this one:

Take a piece of paper and draw a line down the centre of

the page. On one half write a number of general negative sentences about yourself. Add to these during the course of the next day or two as things come into your mind. After a few days, read through the list again and on the other side of the page transform each sentence into a positive, realistic, statement about yourself.

For example: I am always late	I have got to work on time three times this week.
I am argumentative	I have had two arguments this week.
I am shy	I don't like to initiate conversations with people I do not know.
I am skinny	I'm slim!
I'm fat	I'm cuddly!
I'm a nagger	I am persistent
I'm nosey	I find people and their different lives fascinating.

When this second list is complete re-read it and with two different coloured pens underline:

Firstly the statements about yourself that you are prepared to accept and live with.

Secondly the statements you would prefer to be different. With a *third coloured pen* underline the one you wish to change.

Finally set yourself some realistic goals and start working on them!

Giving Criticism to Others

Self-Help Groups

Exercise 1
Find a partner and have a bit of fun criticising each other's clothes in a fairly lighthearted manner. If you like what the other person is wearing, imagine that you don't but remember the hints on pages 58.

Exercise II
Divide into small groups and put a chair in the centre. Each person can practise giving criticism to an imaginary person on the chair. The rest of the group must check that the criticism is constructive and specific.

Exercise III
Please note, this exercise is suitable for groups who have known each other for a while and where a good deal of mutual trust has been built up.

Divide into small groups of between three to five people. Take it in turns to give criticism to each other. The observers should keep the hints given earlier at hand and check that the criticizers are being helpful and as constructive as possible. For the time being the person being criticized should not answer back. There will be plenty of time to defend youselves in later sessions! Finish this session with sharing positive comments about each other.

Individuals: Think about several people you would like to criticize and choose the least risky situation to work on. Using the hints on pages 57–8 note down what it is you want to say to the other person and at the next suitable opportunity have a go. Please note, make sure you have a great reward lined up for yourself afterwards!

Practical Work on Chapter 6

Receiving Criticism

Self-Help Groups

In groups of three to four people practise the skills of NEGATIVE ASSERTION, FOGGING and NEGATIVE ENQUIRY. Each group should decide for themselves if they wish to choose real life situations or hypothetical scenes to role play. Alternatively if you are a very close and mutually trusting group you could take the opportunity to give some genuine criticism. Remember, however, the exercise is in *taking* criticism and not in giving it, so the critic should not bother too much about the way he gives the criticism. It is important to find out exactly what kind of criticism renders each individual unassertive and work in that area. It is, after all, pointless to practise receiving criticism about the way you dress if that kind of feedback doesn't bother you in the slightest. I'm afraid this is the time to expose your Achilles heels if you genuinely want to change your behaviour!

Sometimes people have difficulty in giving criticism. If this happens try having two critics and a fourth person to act as observer and help the recipient respond with the right technique.

Individuals: Draw a line down the centre of a page and on one side jot down a list of typical criticisms people make of you, or you fear they may make of you in the future. On the other side, put down a response using Fogging, Negative Enquiry or Negative Assertion.

Criticism	Assertive Reply
'You look very peaky'	'Yes, you may be right, I don't look my best' (Fogging)
'You are selfish'	'Yes, it is true that I am giving my own needs some priority now' (Negative Assertion)
'Your hair is a mess'	'Do you think the style doesn't suit me?' (Negative Enquiry)

Add to your list over the next few weeks and when you feel confident that you have mastered the techniques, try them out in a relatively safe situation.

Chapter 14

Practical Work on Chapter 7 Getting Prepared

Scripting

Self-Help Groups

Divide into pairs or small groups and after an initial discussion select a problem which would be suitable for scripting. It is always more rewarding to choose a real life problem but if this is not possible here are some suggestions:

1. Asking for a rise at work.

2. Telling your mother that you don't wish to spend Christmas with her.

3. Asking your G.P. for clarification on your problem or the side-effects of treatment.

4. Complaining to a builder about delayed or shoddy work.

5. Asking other members of the family to take a fairer share of housework.

6. Telling a friend that you want more privacy.

When you have finished the scripts, share them in the large

group. Be sure to check that you have included the four main components.

Individuals: Do as above but preferably with the help of a friend. Write out at least six scripts to ensure that the format becomes firmly implanted in your mind. When you are feeling brave try them out!

Visual Aids
Make a poster outlining the main components of a script. For example,

---

Even Fish Need Confidence

Explanation
- objective
- brief
- no theories

Feelings
- acknowledge own feelings
- empathize

Needs
Be selective
Be realistic
Be prepared to compromise

Consequences
- rewards
- punishments

Role Play

Self-Help Groups

Read the section on Role-Play in Chapter 7 very carefully and follow through step-by-step each of the stages. You may find that as your group gets to know each other very well that you may not need to stick rigidly to this model. You may even develop your own method which may be just as effective.

Don't forget that role-play sessions need not be heavy and very dramatic to be effective. In our groups they have always been a great source of fun as well as enlightenment.

Individuals: If you have any interested friends or family, why not try to do a role-play as outlined in Chapter 7.

If not, run through a variety of scenes in your head and allow your imagination to help you rehearse your roles.

If the scene involves only a few people you can act each part yourself.

Alternatively, you could use some of your newly acquired assertive skills to set up your own self-help group!

Chapter 15
Some Suggestions for Further Study

Booklist

Smith, Manuel J., *When I say No, I Feel Guilty*. (Bantam Books, 1976).

Bower, Sharon Anthony and Bower, Gordon H., *Asserting Yourself: A Practical Guide for Positive Change*. (Addison-Wesley Publishing Co. 1976).

Kelley, Colleen, *Assertion Training – a Facilitator's Guide*. (University Associates, 1979).

Dickson, Anne, *A Woman in Your Own Right*. (Quartet Books, 1982).

Lindenfield, Gael and Adams, Robert, *Problem Solving Through Self-Help Groups*. (Self-Help Associates, 1984).

Townend, Anni, *Assertion Training: – A Handbook for those Involved in Training*. (Family Planning Association Education Unit, 1986).

Baer, Jean, *How to be an Assertive (Not Aggressive) Woman in Life, in Love, & on the Job!* The Total Guide to Self-Assertiveness. (New American Library, 1976).

Kelley, Jan D., and Winship, Barbara J., *I am Worth It*. (Nelson-Hall, 1979).

Dyer, Wayne W., *Pulling Your Own Strings*. (Avon Books, 1979).

Alberti, R. E., and Emmons, M. L., *Stand Up, Speak Out, Talk Back!* (Pocket Books, 1984).

Courses

An increasing number of short courses in Assertiveness Training are now being run. Many trainers work freelance and may be able to design a course to suit the particular needs of your group.

Contact the following places for details of any local courses:

- Adult Education Departments
- Departments of Psychology at Universities and Polytechnics
- Local Associations of Mental Health
- Libraries

My own courses usually take place in Leeds or Ilkley, although I have been known to travel a little further afield. If you live locally I would be happy to inform you of any courses and trainers I know of in the area.

I hope that you will find this self-help programme helpful. Any queries, please do not hesitate to contact me care of the publishers. Comments and suggestions would also be very welcome!

Finally, design an attractive and colourful poster for yourself using the word CONFIDENCE as a constant reminder of the important elements of assertiveness. Alternatively, photocopy page 9 and pin it up in a prominent place.

GOOD LUCK!

Index